# The Desert Chief

## STORY OF THUMAMA IBN UTHAL

Khurram Murad

THE ISLAMIC FOUNDATION

# MUSLIM CHILDREN'S LIBRARY SERIES

ISBN 0 86037 136 0

## MUSLIM CHILDREN'S LIBRARY

**General Editors**
Khurram Murad and Mashuq Ally

**THE DESERT CHIEF**
Author: Khurram Murad
Illustrations: Latifa Ahmad
Editing: Mardijah A. Tarantino

These stories are about the Prophet and his Companions and, though woven
around authentic ahadith, should be regarded only as stories.

*Published by*
The Islamic Foundation, Markfield Dawah Centre,
Ratby Lane, Markfield, Leicester LE67 9RN, United Kingdom

Quran House, P.O. Box 30611, Nairobi, Kenya

P.M.B. 3193, Kano, Nigeria

*British Library Cataloguing in Publication Data*
Murad, Khurram
The Desert Chief.—(Muslim children's library; 14)
1. Muhammad (Prophet)—Juvenile literature
I. Title    II. Islamic Foundation    III. Series
297'.63    BP75.

ISBN 0-86037-136-0

# MUSLIM CHILDREN'S LIBRARY

### An Introduction

Here is a new series of books, but with a difference, for children of all ages. Published by the Islamic Foundation, the Muslim Children's Library has been produced to provide young people with something they cannot perhaps find anywhere else.

Most of today's children's books aim only to entertain and inform or to teach some necessary skills, but not to develop the inner and moral resources. Entertainment and skills by themselves impart nothing of value to life unless a child is also helped to discover deeper meaning in himself and the world around him. Yet there is no place in them for God, who alone gives meaning to life and the universe, nor for the divine guidance brought by His prophets, following which can alone ensure an integrated development of the total personality.

Such books, in fact, rob young people of access to true knowledge. They give them no unchanging standards of right and wrong, nor any incentives to live by what is right and refrain from what is wrong. The result is that all too often the young enter adult life in a state of social alienation and bewilderment, unable to cope with the seemingly unlimited choices of the world around them. The situation is especially devastating for the Muslim child as he may grow up cut off from his culture and values.

The Muslim Children's Library aspires to remedy this deficiency by showing children the deeper meaning of life and the world around them; by pointing them along the paths leading to an integrated development of all aspects of their personality; by helping to give them the capacity to cope with the complexities of their world, both personal and social; by opening vistas into a world extending far beyond this life; and, to a Muslim child especially, by providing a fresh and strong faith, a dynamic commitment, an indelible sense of identity, a throbbing yearning and an urge to struggle, all rooted in Islam.

The books aim to help a child anchor his development on the rock of divine guidance, and to understand himself and relate to himself and others in just and meaningful ways. They relate directly to his soul and intellect, to his emotions and imagination, to his motives and desires, to his anxieties and hopes — indeed, to every aspect of his fragile, but potentially rich personality. At the same time it is recognised that for a book to hold a child's attention, he must enjoy reading it; it should therefore arouse his curiosity and entertain him as well. The style, the language, the illustrations and the production of the books are all geared to this goal. They provide moral education, but not through sermons or ethical abstractions.

Although these books are based entirely on Islamic teachings and the vast Muslim heritage, they should be of equal interest and value to all children, whatever their country or creed; for Islam is a universal religion, the natural path.

Adults, too, may find much of use in them. In particular, Muslim parents and teachers will find that they provide what they have for so long been so badly needing. The books will include texts on the Quran, the Sunnah and other basic sources and teachings of Islam, as well as history, stories and anecdotes for supplementary reading. Each book will cater for a particular age group, classified into: pre-school, 5-8 years, 8-11, 11-14 and 14-17.

We invite parents and teachers to use these books in homes and classrooms, at breakfast tables and bedside and encourage children to derive maximum benefit from them. At the same time their greatly valued observations and suggestions are highly welcome.

To the young reader we say: you hold in your hands books which may be entirely different from those you have been reading till now, but we sincerely hope you will enjoy them; try, through these books, to understand yourself, your life, your experiences and the universe around you. They will open before your eyes new paths and models in life that you will be curious to explore and find exciting and rewarding to follow. May God be with you forever.

And may He bless with His mercy and acceptance our humble contribution to the urgent and gigantic task of producing books for a new generation of people, a task which we have undertaken in all humility and hope.

**Director General**

In the sixth year after the Hijra, the Prophet Muhammad (Peace and Blessings be upon him)* sent letters to all the chiefs and kings of countries within reach of Arabia, inviting them to Islam. Some, like Heraclius, the Emperor of Rome, read the letter and considered the invitation seriously, but was prevented from embracing Islam by his own weaknesses. He was not even prepared to follow Christianity . . . much less embrace some unknown Arab merchant . . . that, too, at the risk of losing the support of his generals and priests and possibly losing his throne!

Parvaiz, or Chosroes, the mighty king of Persia, disdainfully tore the letter in shreds in the presence of the envoy who had brought it, and instructed the governor of his Arabian province of Yemen, Badhan, to go and teach a lesson to the madman of Madina who dared to write him such a letter. The Negus of Abyssinia, on the other hand, who had earlier welcomed Muslims to his country and provided them with refuge, was ready to accept the invitation to embrace Islam.

Amongst the chiefs to whom the letter was sent, was one named Thumama, chief of the Banu Hanifa in

*Muslims are required to invoke Allah's blessings and peace upon the Prophet whenever his name is mentioned.

# A   HISTORIC   DOCUMENT

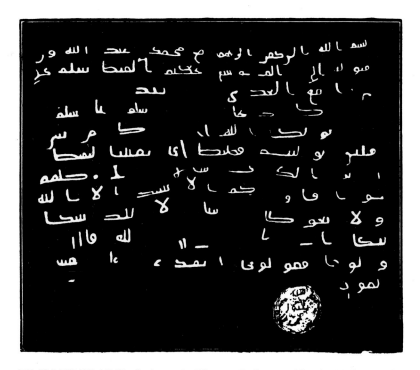

**P**HOTOGRAPH *of a letter in Khatt-e-Kufi signed by the Holy Prophet to "Mukavkis" Byzantinian King of Egypt in the year 7 of Hijra. The letter reads:–*

*"This letter is for Mukavkis, the King of Copts, from God's servant and from Prophet Muhammad. After greetings to those who accept the guidance of God, I invite you to adopt "Kalima-e-Shahadet" which is a form of Islamic prayer.*

*Accept Islam, you will be safe and God will grant you rewards and compensations. If you refuse and reject, the sins and faults of Copts, your subject, will be visited on you.*

*O Believers in the Books, accept the Kalima which means the same thing to you as to us: we do not worship any but the Almighty God; we do not accept that he has any partner and we do not consider that some one of us is God.*

*If the Kalima puts you on the right path, say that we are witness that you are real believers in God and are Muslims."*

MUHAMMAD, Prophet of God.

The original of this letter is preserved in the library of Coptic monks village Ahmin in Egypt.

Yamama in Najd. Thumama, up until then, had heard about Muhammad, but had avoided having any dealings with Muslims one way or another. He was not going to get involved in petty squabbles between the Quraysh and one of their rebellious sons. But when the invitation to join Islam came to him personally, he was outraged.

'Why that renegade dares to address *me*, Thumama, Chief of the Banu Hanifa, to join his bunch of nonsensical heretics? How *dare* he? Who does he take me for? This shall not pass unnoticed. He has been a thorn in the side of the Quraysh for some time. This insult provides me with an excuse to wipe him out. Then we shall hear no more of heretical messages and insulting invitations.'

From that day, Thumama began scheming and plotting to kill the Blessed Prophet. He and his men never missed an opportunity to attack him or try to ambush him. Most of the attempts failed because of the vigilance of the Blessed Prophet's Companions, although one attempt would have succeeded if a distant uncle of Thumama's, a Muslim, had not, at the last moment, got word to the Blessed Prophet, thereby saving his life.

This did not stop Thumama. He continued raiding and attacking the Muslims and when his men were clever enough to ambush one, they were ordered to inflict on him a slow, painful death. The Blessed

Prophet was left no alternative but to pronounce a death sentence upon Thumama, which meant that if ever he were caught by the Muslims, he would be put to death.

The time came for the annual Pilgrimage to Makka. Thumama used to make the journey alone, from Yamama to Makka; he knew that wherever he stopped on the way he would be an honoured guest. For the times when he had to set up camp alone, he was amply stocked with food and supplies besides the usual offerings needed for the sacrifice to his idols.

One evening he found himself off the usual path and, although he did not realise it, close to Madina. As night fell, he prepared to make camp. He unfolded his bedding, placed a water bag by his head and built up the small fire he had made to keep off wild animals. Finally, he settled down and was soon asleep.

Not far away, a party of Muslims set out on patrol from Madina in search of spies and enemies. These intruders, if given a chance, would plunder, loot and kill the Muslims; so the Blessed Prophet had organised these patrols as a means of protection.

The night was as black as ink. There was not a star in the sky, nor the moon yet risen, when the patrol came over a hill and spotted the glowing embers of

Thumama's camp-fire. 'Approach with caution', advised the leader of the party as they stealthily crept forward. When they had surrounded the camp, the leader called out:

'You there. Get up and identify yourself!'

Thumama leapt up and reached for his sword, but seeing himself surrounded, settled down again.

'Your name and identity', repeated the leader. 'Where are you heading? What is your business here?'

Thumama was beginning to realise who the men were; he certainly was not going to give his name at any cost.

'Where do you come from, your name?'

Still, Thumama refused to answer.

'Then if you won't answer our questions, we can only suspect you are here for the wrong reasons. Come with us.'

Thumama was a fearless man and very proud. He stood up with dignity, folded his belongings and walked off in front of them as if he were going by his own choice. The patrol was made up of Ansars who were not at all familiar with the Yamamites. They had no idea that they had arrested a high chief of the Banu Hanifa, one of their fiercest enemies!

'If he is a spy', said one, 'the Blessed Prophet will tell us what to do with him'.

Arriving at Madina, they led Thumama to the mosque and tied him to one of the pillars.

Soon after dawn, the Blessed Prophet came from his home to the mosque, noticed the prisoner tied to a pillar and immediately recognised Thumama. The patrol had been waiting all this time to find out who it was they had arrested.

'This is Thumama, Chief of the Bani Hanifa of Yamama', he told the Companions.

If they did not know him by sight, they certainly recognised the name.

'He who treacherously murdered our brothers and plotted time after time to kill you?'

'Yes', replied the Blessed Prophet, and to the surprise of the Companions, he added: 'And I want you to treat him well.'

He then walked by Thumama without saying a word and began to lead the Prayers.

Thus Thumama, whether he wanted to or not, witnessed for the first time the Muslim Prayers and heard the recitations of the Quran.

The first thing the Blessed Prophet did upon returning to his quarters, which led directly into the mosque, was to ask his family to prepare the very best food they had and to milk the she-camel every morning and evening so that Thumama would have plenty of fresh milk.

One of the Companions was then asked to untie Thumama's hands so that he could eat some of the delicious food. The Companion could not believe his eyes when he saw the meal which the Blessed Prophet had ordered for his enemy. 'I thought we would be ordered to execute him, not feed him like a king', he exclaimed to the others.

After Thumama had eaten his fill, the Blessed Prophet came to see him and said:

'Now, Thumama, what do you have to say?'

Thumama, who had really enjoyed his meal, looked up at the Blessed Prophet with a little more respect: 'Muhammad, all is well with me. If you kill me, then so be it. If you show me kindness, I shall be grateful. If it is wealth and riches you need, I can provide them. The choice, of course, is yours', answered Thumama, in a calm voice.

Thumama was prepared to accept his fate with dignity. But the Blessed Prophet left him without saying a word and did not speak to him again for two days, during which time he ordered that Thumama be served the very best food and fresh camel milk.

On the third day, the Blessed Prophet approached him again.

'Well, Thumama, what have you to say to me?'

'Look, Muhammad', he answered, 'it is like this: I am prepared to die, if that is what you decide; if you continue treating me as you have been doing, I shall be grateful. And if it is money you want, you know full well that I can provide you with a generous ransom. There you have it.'

The Blessed Prophet stood looking at him for a moment and then, without replying, walked off.

Another day came and went. Thumama began to feel more like a guest than a prisoner. Not only had he been given excellent meals worthy of the chief that he was, but he had been entertained daily by the gatherings and Prayers of the Blessed Prophet and his Companions. 'It is not so bad after all, being a prisoner of this curious man. At least he is a man of honour, from what I see.'

The next day the Blessed Prophet returned and once again asked Thumama the same question:

'Thumama, what have you to say now?'

Thumama couldn't figure out what the Blessed Prophet wanted of him. 'Don't you understand what

I am saying, Muhammad? I repeat that I am at your service. You may kill me, feed me, or ask for my wealth. It is all the same to me.'

'Alright', answered the Blessed Prophet, and, turning to the Companions, ordered: 'Let him go.'

Two men came forward, untied Thumama's wrists, and released him. Thumama was dumbfounded. What kind of a man was this? Did he not realise that he, Thumama, had scorned his letter, killed his men, and plotted many times to take his life? Thumama took a step forward, and the Companions, who surrounded him, made way for him to walk off a free man.

Upon reaching the outskirts of the city, he was no longer so sure of himself. It was as if his whole world had been turned around and the direction of his life pointed elsewhere. He felt like a different man. He walked on until he reached a garden with a cool spring and a grove of trees, where he sat down for a moment, trying to collect his thoughts.

He had no desire to return to his home. Nor did he any longer feel hatred for the Blessed Prophet and his followers. He had absolutely no wish to go anywhere except back to where he had just come from, the Blessed Prophet's Mosque!

Leaning over the cool stream, he carefully

performed ablutions as he had seen the Companions doing. Then, adjusting his clothes as neatly as possible, and smoothing down his beard, he walked with a firm step back to the Blessed Prophet's Mosque.

Some Companions saw him coming.

'Isn't that Thumama coming this way?' they called to the others.

Thumama looked neither right or left. Stepping forward into the assembly, he faced the Blessed Prophet and announced:

'I, Thumama, Chief of the Banu Hanifa of Yamama, declare and witness there is but One God and you, Muhammad, are His Messenger.'

The Companions looked at one another with surprise and joy.

'Muhammad', continued Thumama, 'by God there was no face on this earth which I hated more than yours, and now there is none that I love more. Of all the religions, yours I despised the most, and now there is none other I would rather give my life for. Yes, and there was no city I abhorred more than this one, your city of Madina, and now I find it the dearest of all cities, because it is the home of my Beloved Prophet and his Companions . . . Muhammad . . . ' and here Thumama's voice dropped and he became more humble.

'I have shed the blood of many of your followers. How will I ever atone for that?'

The Blessed Prophet answered simply: 'There lies no blame on you, Thumama. Indeed, Islam erases all the sins that a person has committed previously. You have been awarded the highest of awards, that of entering Islam. There could not have been greater mercy or grace bestowed upon you.'

Thumama's face radiated joy and gratefulness at these words. Placing his hand on his breast he vowed: 'By God, from now on I pledge my life, my property and my soul to help you bring idol worshippers to Islam, and those that refuse I shall pursue more fiercely than I did your followers.'

He now dropped his hand, and resumed in a more normal tone. 'Messenger of God, when your patrol arrested me, I was going on Pilgrimage to Makka. What shall I do now?'

'You shall go on Pilgrimage', answered the Blessed Prophet, 'but not to the idols which you now know to be worthless. Come, I shall show you how to perform the Pilgrimage according to Islam.' And so saying, the Blessed Prophet instructed Thumama in the verses and actions and postures for the occasion.

Shortly after this, Thumama arrived in Makka. As he made his way through the streets to the heart of the town, he announced loudly what he had learned from the Blessed Prophet:

'I come at Your bidding, O Lord, I come at Your bidding! I come at Your bidding! There is none like unto You. I come at Your bidding! All praise and bounty belong to You, and the Kingdoms of the heavens and earth too. And there is none like unto You.'

In so doing, Thumama was one of those Muslims who entered Makka openly declaring his intention of performing the lesser Pilgrimage of Ka'ba, the Umrah.

What a stir Thumama's cry caused in Makka that day! Men rushed from their houses to see what the commotion was. Some, when they heard the announcement, came brandishing their swords and threatened to attack him. But Thumama completely ignored their threats. As one young man lunged at him, an elder of the Quraysh stopped his hand.

'Idiot!' he cried, 'do you not see who it is? It is Thumama himself of the Banu Hanifa . . . if you damage a hair of his beard the grain supplies to Makka will be stopped.'

Some of the elders approached Thumama and tried to reason with him:

'Look, Thumama, what has happened to you? We cannot believe that you have given up the religion of your forefathers . . . how did you get led astray like this?'

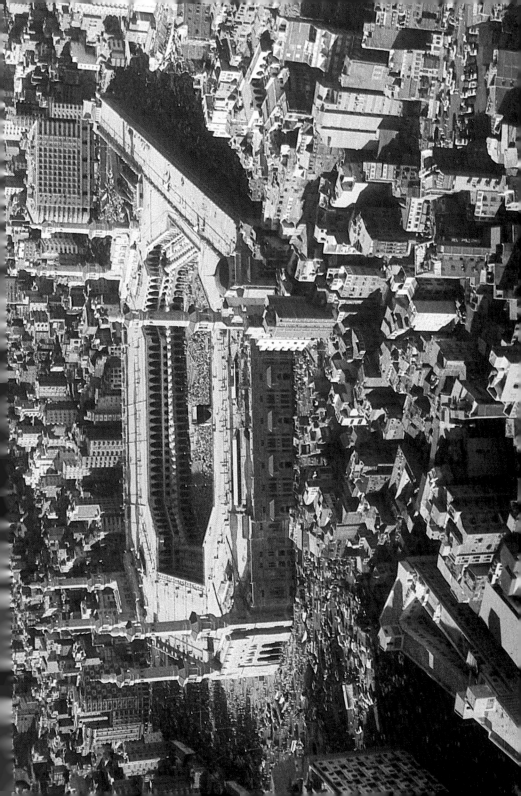

Thumama turned on them with head held high. 'Indeed! I have found the best of all religions! Muhammad's religion, the religion of Islam! And furthermore' . . . for he had seen his advantage . . . 'if you all do not join me in the worship of the One God, not a single grain of wheat from Yamama will grace your tables, for I shall instruct my tribe to block all supplies to Makka!'

This is exactly what the Quraysh feared; so, after shaking their heads and muttering among themselves, they said:

'Go ahead, then Thumama . . . we do not want you to block the grain supplies . . . but allow us at least to cover our ears while you shout the heresy Muhammad has taught you!' And so they let him pass.

Thumama performed the Umrah as he had been taught to do by the Blessed Prophet, praying to the One God instead of to the many gods he had served before. But he noticed that not one Quraysh had come to join him in Prayers or to announce their intention to follow the new religion. Thumama was a man of his word and always kept his promises whatever they were and to whomever they were made. So upon arriving in Yamama, he gave orders to stop all shipments of grain to Makka.

Gradually the blockade began to take effect. Supplies of grain began to dwindle and prices rose

steadily day by day. Finally, there was no grain to be had in Makka, nor any bread on any table, even the wealthy Quraysh began to go hungry. The people of Makka began to panic. If Thumama kept this up, even the children would go hungry and eventually starve to death.

While conscious of the persecution and torture which they had brought upon the Blessed Prophet and his people, they were forced to swallow their pride and ask him to intervene. They sent the following message to Madina:

'You try to always set the example of being kind to relatives. You urge the young to be merciful. Yet you have not only slain the fathers of this city with the sword, you would allow their children to die of hunger. We implore you to stop the blockade or our children will starve.'

As a result of this, the Blessed Prophet wrote to Thumama, and Thumama, only because the Blessed Prophet urged him to, ordered the supply of grain to be continued. 'Only because of the Blessed Prophet's order do I break my word', he declared.

This was an example of how the Blessed Prophet showed mercy and kindness to his enemies. How he won the heart of a die-hard enemy like Thumama.